West

Walks

Hugh Stoker

*with sketch maps and
photographs by the author*

By the same author:

SOUTH DORSET WALKS
EAST DEVON WALKS
WILDTRACK WALKS IN WEST DORSET
SEA FISHING IN DORSET
SEA FISHING IN HAMPSHIRE & ISLE OF WIGHT
THE MODERN SEA ANGLER
A MANUAL OF SEA FISHING BAITS
COMPLETE GUIDE TO SEA FISHING
SEA ANGLING HOTSPOTS

First published 1982
Second impression (revised) 1983
Third impression (revised) 1984
Fourth impression (revised) 1986
Fifth impression (revised) 1989
Sixth impression (revised) 1991
Seventh impression (revised) 1993
Eighth impression (revised) 1996
Ninth impression (revised) 1998
Tenth impression (revised) 2000

ISBN 0 9508088 0 6

CONTENTS

4

Introduction

WEST DORSET is criss-crossed by a veritable maze of public footpaths, bridleways, cliff tracks, forest trails, prehistoric ridgeways, ancient drove roads and packhorse trails. To deal with them all in this pocket-sized booklet would be quite impossible, so instead I have concentrated on my "Top Twenty" favourite walks – the ones which have given me most pleasure during the fifty-odd years I have been living in this delightful corner of Dorset.

Most of the walks follow a circular route, beginning and ending at a spot where the motorist can conveniently park his car without causing an obstruction. As for the walks themselves, their main objective is to seek out the beautiful and secluded places, where you are most likely to see the *real* Dorset, and the wild creatures that live in it.

All the routes described are easily within the average walker's capabilities, but they *are* cross-country walks, and suitable footwear is therefore essential. The best choice for all seasons is a pair of sturdy, water-repellent walking boots with non-slip cleated soles – worn, of course, with thick woollen socks. However, on the upland walks in dry summer weather you may prefer lightweight boots or heavily cleated walking shoes. Smooth-soled shoes should be avoided at all costs; they are slippery on grass, and can be dangerous on the steep hill slopes and cliff paths of West Dorset.

Although sketch maps have been included in this book, a fairly large-scale Ordnance Survey map will also prove useful, as well as adding considerably to the enjoyment and interest of your walk. The best choice is one of the 1:25000 series, which show all public rights-of-way and field boundaries. (See next page for further information).

An inexpensive pocket compass will also come in handy, particularly when exploring some of the more remote and seldom-used routes. The coastal walks are obviously well-trodden, and the paths clearly defined. On many inland walks, however, there may be no visible path when crossing grassy fields and meadows – just the stiles and gateways linking various sections of a right of way. On these "off-the-beaten-track" sections I have purposely made my directions more explicit, and where necessary have included simple compass bearings. You will find these particularly useful when your next objective – be it stile, footbridge or gateway – happens to be hidden on the far side of a hill, or behind overhanging tree branches.

Finally, do please observe the Country Code when sampling these walks. Don't park your car where it will obstruct a narrow lane, or prevent tractors and trailers manoeuvring into a field gateway. If you have a dog, keep it under control at all times. Keep it on a lead when walking in sheep country, or near woodland game reserves. Enjoy yourselves!

IMPORTANT NOTE:
ORDNANCE SURVEY MAPS

Since the publication of previous editions of this book, the Ordnance Survey have introduced two types of 1:25000 maps that are ideal for walkers. Known as the "Explorer" and "Outdoor Leisure" series, they provide much wider coverage than the earlier "Pathfinder" maps. We therefore now recommend the following:

Explorer sheet 116 for Walks 1 – 15 and 20;

Pathfinder sheet 1317 for Walks 16 – 19.

Walk No. 1
The Undercliff Nature Reserve
Distance: Optional (5 – 14 miles).
O.S. Map Nos: SY 29/39 (1:25000) or 193 (1:50000)

THE coastal cliffs on either side of Lyme Regis are very unstable, and subject to frequent landslips and rock falls. This is caused by underground water beneath the porous greensand loosening a sloping foundation of

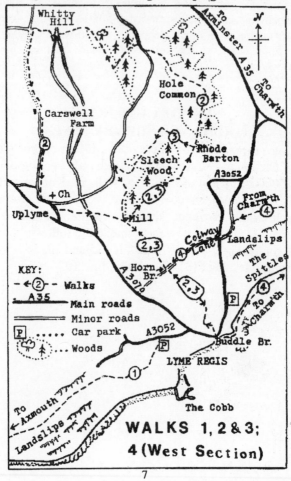

KEY:
- –←②– – Walks
- A35 — Main roads
- ═══ — Minor roads
- P ⋯ — Car park
- 🌲 ⋯ — Woods

WALKS 1, 2 & 3;
4 (West Section)

slippery clay, which then oozes slowly downhill, carrying its top-burden with it.

Occasionally — usually after a prolonged period of wet weather — a landslip occurs of truly vast proportions. Perhaps the most memorable one took place at Christmas, 1839, when over half a mile of cliff-top land near Dowlands, 3½ miles west of Lyme Regis, slipped down overnight to open up a chasm hundreds of feet deep.

Smaller and less spectacular landslips occur every year all along this stretch of coast, and the overall length of the undercliff area is approximately 5 miles, and covers some 800 acres. Over the years a dense growth of trees and shrubs has sprung up, forming a sort of English "jungle" which is now the Axmouth - Lyme Regis National Nature Reserve. The public footpath which meanders through this most unusual wilderness is definitely well-worth exploring.

Needless to say, badgers, foxes and many other forms of wild life abound in the reserve, and some 400 species of wild flowers have been recorded. It should be mentioned, however, that the path becomes muddy and slippery in places during wet weather, so stout boots are advisable.

Although most of the walks described in this book have been planned to provide you with a circular route, this is unfortunately not practical within the narrow confines of the nature reserve. The majority of visitors are content to walk westwards from Lyme along the undercliff trail for as far as their energy and personal inclination dictate, and then simply turn round and retrace their steps.

Alternatively, you could perhaps get a lift by road to Axmouth, and from there walk the entire length of the footpath back to Lyme — a total distance of about 7 - 8 miles. At the Axmouth end the path begins by approaching the cliff-top via the golf course, and then after a mile or so it descends into the wooded nature reserve.

The most convenient place in Lyme from which to start the walk is the large car park at the top end of Cobb Road. From the lower SW corner of the car park a short cul-de-sac road leads on to a grassy hillside overlooking the sea. From here a field path wanders off in a westerly direction, leading you gently uphill to join a narrow by-lane which peters out after about a ¼ mile upon reaching Underhill Farm.

At the end of the lane a footpath enters the nature reserve. From here onwards the trail is well-defined, and after 2½ miles takes you past the grounds of Allhallows School. There can be few other schools in the country enjoying such a pleasant longshore situation. Among other things, the school has its own official cliff rescue team, manned by a master and some of the senior boys.

Incidentally, I first walked this undercliff path one scorching hot August day in 1932. I was 12 years old at the time, and holidaying in Seaton with my recently widowed mother. I recall that in those days the undergrowth bordering the path was much less dense than it is now, and in several herbage-carpeted woodland glades we came upon large concentrations of Adonis Blue butterflies.

Our objective on that walk was the famous "Landslip Cottage", which in those days stood beside the path in a delightful tree-embowered garden. Here two elderly ladies used to serve teas to the hundreds of ramblers who travelled the undercliff trail in summer.

I remember the standard charge for one of their teas was one shilling per person — 5 pence in today's currency. For that princely sum we were given a large family-sized pot of tea, a piled dishful of home-made scones and strawberry jam, and a generous assortment of cakes and buns.... as many as even a hungry 12 year old boy could wish for!

An interesting story used to be told about "Landslip Cottage". Apparently it had originally stood some distance back from the cliff-edge, but one morning many years previously its occupants had woken up to find that

9

overnight a massive landslip had moved their home hundreds of feet, and it now stood upright and almost undamaged in a newly-formed bit of the undercliff "No-man's-land"!

The cottage I remember so vividly no longer stands beside the path. Over the years a long succession of further landslips and subsidences has carried it inexorably downhill into a more precarious situation. Abandoned by its occupants, the cottage and its little sun-trap of a garden were eventually overwhelmed by the encroaching "jungle".

Walk No. 2
A Thatched Watermill and a Woodland Trail
Lyme Regis — Sleech Wood — Hole Common — Whitty Hill — Uplyme — Sleech Wood — Lyme Regis
Distance: Approx. 8 miles.
O.S. Map: SY 29/39 (1: 25000) or 193 (1:50000)

THE Buddle Bridge, which crosses the River Lim where it flows into the sea, makes a convenient starting point for this walk. This is the oldest part of Lyme — a place of narrow, winding streets and shadowy alleyways — and as long ago as Saxon times a small community of fisherfolk and "salt-boilers" lived here beside the banks of the Lim.

From Buddle Bridge it is only a few yards to Coombe Street. A little way up this street you turn off on to a footpath immediately alongside the "Ship Inn". This takes you past an old watermill, and then on to a raised footpath with the rushing River Lim on your left hand and the old mill leat on your right.

On the far bank of the river, and accessible by a footbridge, is a small public garden containing the Leper's Well — a moss-grown stone basin set in an ancient archway. About 700 years ago a leper hospital stood near this spot, and tradition has it that this well was used by its inhabitants.

Continuing along the raised footpath (which is known as "the Lynch") you come to Goslings Bridge and the very picturesque stretch of riverside known as Mill Green. Incidentally, until the late 1700's, this narrow riverside lane was the only way out of Lyme for wheeled traffic — all other routes being virtually impassible except on foot, horseback, or by pack pony.

The lane heads upstream past a roaring weir, and soon brings you out on to a narrow by-road which used to be the main highway between Exeter and Dorchester. It crosses the River Lim at this point by an interesting old bridge which has a single steeply pointed arch. It is known as Horn Bridge — so-called, according to some, because mail coach drivers used to sound their post horns here to demand a clearway when negotiating the steep hills which flank the bridge on either side.

Heading straight on across this by-road, you now follow a hard-surfaced cart track which keeps close company with the river until you come to a whitewashed farmhouse. Leaving the farm track here, you bear away to the left along a footpath which crosses the river by a footbridge just below another weir.

The footpath now leads you across a grassy meadow to a picturesque thatched watermill — its waterwheel unfortunately now permanently idle. The mill is situated on the edge of a dense expanse of forest which rejoices in the intriguing name of Sleech Wood.

The public footpath skirts the eastern edge of the mill cottage garden, and then immediately afterwards forks in two directions — left on to a bridleway which follows the W side of Sleech Wood, and to the right around the SE corner of the wood.

On this walk you take the right-hand fork. This path takes you through the narrow S end of Sleech Wood and then, after passing the perimeter fence of a tiny sewage works, passes through a gate into a grassy field. With Sleech Wood over on your left, head NE across this field until you come to another gate. Pass through this into the next field. Keep Sleech Wood on your left for about 200 yards; then bear right (E) towards a gate which brings you out on to an unsurfaced farm road — classified as a public footpath.

Turn left along this road, ignoring waymarks pointing off to the right and left. Soon you'll come to Rhode Barton Farm, and here the right of way curves sharp left around the garden of a house, and then immediately afterwards curves right again (NNE) — at the same time dwindling into a narrow track overhung with trees. You now have a field on your left and some woodland on your right. For a short distance this track becomes muddy after rain, but very soon the going becomes firmer as the path leads you into an extensive tract of woodland known as Hole Common. This, to my way of thinking, is the best part of the walk.

Eventually the path joins up with a broad forestry track. Turn right (NW) along this until you come to a gate on the far side of a vehicle turning place. Pass through the gate into a grassy field flanked on three sides by thick woodland. A tiny tributary of the River Lim flows along the bottom of this field and marks the boundary between Dorset and Devon.

Keeping the stream on your left, continue along its bank for about 50 yards until you come to a footbridge. After crossing this bridge into Devon, head up a grassy field, keeping the hedge close on your left-hand side. Soon you'll come to a gate leading on to a tarred by-lane. Turn right for about 150 yards; then turn left up a side-track leading to "The Haven" and "Haven Cottage".

This lane soon ends alongside these cottages, and from there you continue along a public footpath (not waymarked) which dives abruptly into a beautiful tract of hillside woodland. At first the path may be muddy underfoot, but it soon becomes drier as it climbs up the steep hillside. Heading in a roughly SW direction, but with several twists and turns, this pleasant wildtrack path eventually emerges into a narrow grassy field. Continue SW along the bottom of this field; then turn right (NNW) and follow the hedge to a stile at the far end of the field.

After crossing the stile, continue NNW along a path which offers a fine panoramic view of West Dorset away on your right. Soon the path enters a pine plantation, and near the far end of this wood a stile leads out into a grassy field. This is the summit of Whitty Hill, over 650 feet high. Now bear WSW, aiming for the far right-hand corner of the field where another stile brings you out on to a by-lane. Cross this lane and turn SSW down a nearby fork for just a few yards until you come to a signposted footpath leading off to the right (NW) alongside a small dwelling called "Sunshine Cottage".

Skirting around the rear of the cottage, the path leads you downhill into a hollow below a farmhouse. Bear left (W) across this hollow and pass through a nearby gate. Ahead, at the top of a rise and to your right, you'll see a gate with a stile alongside it. Cross this stile into the next field and follow the left-hand hedge until you come to a gate leading out on to a tarred by-lane.

Turn left (S) down this lane for just a few yards until it bends sharply to the right. Here you continue straight on (S) along an unsurfaced bridleway which leads downhill past Carsewell Farm. Beyond the farm the lane acquires a tarred surface, and on reaching the outskirts of Uplyme you should keep turning left until you reach Uplyme Church.

Directly opposite the church take the right-hand fork which leads down a short steep hill. Near the bottom of this hill, alongside a cottage with the name "Brook Cottage" above the porch, you'll see a footpath leading off to the left. This path follows the River Lim until it brings you to another tarred lane. Directly opposite, a signpost points the way down a bridlepath called Mill Lane. Follow this picturesque tree-draped trail, perched high above the babbling River Lim, and soon you'll find yourself back at the thatched watermill under the lee of Sleech Wood. From this point onwards you follow the river back to Lyme Regis, along the route described in the opening stages of this walk.

Walk No. 3
A Ramble Around Sleech Wood
Lyme Regis — Sleech Wood — Rhode Barton — Lyme Regis

Distance: Approx. 5 miles.

O.S. Map: SY 29/39 (1:25000) or 193 (1:50000)

THIS circular walk can best be described as a shortened version of Walk No. 2, although it offers a bonus by exploring a very pleasant field path not covered on the longer route.

To begin with you should make for the old mill at Sleech Wood, and then head on to Rhode Barton, following the directions given in Walk No. 2

Skirt left around the house at Rhode Barton and head NNE down a rough track over-hung with trees. After about 50 yards you pass through a gate across the lane; then shortly afterwards turn left through a waymarked gate leading into a grassy field. Keeping the wooded field boundary close on your right, head NW downhill until you come to a tree-hidden stream. Turn left (SW) along the stream bank for about 250 yards towards the edge of Sleech Wood. A footbridge crosses this stream, but is completely hidden among dense bushes. However, you'll find it about 50 yards upstream from where the field borders Sleech Wood. Cross bridge and head NW up a grassy slope towards a nearby farmhouse.

As you approach the farmhouse on the other side of the stream you will see a stile immediately ahead of you. DON'T cross this; instead look to your left and you'll see another stile leading into a large grassy field with a line of electricity poles stretching across it. Follow these poles, and in due course you will come to another stile giving access to a woodland path — which in turn leads on to a narrow lane.

Turn left when this lane meets a tarred by-road; then about 100 yards further on, after passing a pink-washed house called "Mulberry", fork left down a pleasant bridleway which curves downhill and runs alongside the W edge of Sleech Wood.

Soon you will arrive back at the old thatched mill beside the River Lim, and from there you can return to Lyme Regis by the route you set out along, keeping close company with the river most of the way.

Points of Interest

Buddle Bridge, which dates from medieval times, was the scene of much smuggling activity in days gone by. Under cover of darkness the local "free-traders" would unload their contraband on the nearby beach, and then spirit it swiftly away by wading under the bridge and up the shallow river-bed beyond. The kegs, or whatever, were then quickly hoisted by rope into the old houses which conveniently back on to the river, forming a deep, secretive canyon of mossy stones and cobwebby windows. On high tides it was even possible to work a small contraband-laden boat under the bridge and up the stream. It is said that much of Lyme's smuggling trade was conducted with Morlaix, in Brittany.

Walk No. 4
Weird Creatures from the Past

Lyme Regis – Charmouth – Lyme Regis
Distance: Approx. 5½ miles
O.S. Maps: Explorer sheet 116 or Pathfinder 1318
(1:25000); 193 (1:50000)
Sketch maps: See pages 7 and 25

AS the first stage of this walk is along the seashore it is essential to cover this section during the latter half of a *falling* tide. The ideal time to choose is about an hour before dead low water, during reasonably calm weather. CONSULT A TIDE TABLE – DO NOT GUESS WHAT THE TIDE IS DOING. People have been drowned in the past through "taking a chance".

Quite apart from the all-important safety factor, you will be walking on a pleasanter surface at low tide – on smooth sand and bed-rock, instead of the loose stones and small boulders that predominate along much of the high water mark.

A convenient starting point for this walk is Buddle Bridge (see page 16). A few yards E, almost opposite the Fossil Shop, you come to Gun Cliff – so-called because cannon used to be mounted here to protect the town from seaborne raiders.

Since publication of previous editions, the old stone walls of Gun Cliff have been reinforced by massive sea defences that also conceal within them a new sewage control station. Your route lies eastwards along this new sea wall until some steps take you down on to the beach.

You now pass below an unstable stretch of grey-hued cliffs called the Spittles – probably because they are always dribbling with tiny rivulets of surface water.

Beyond the Spittles a fine stretch of sand is exposed around low water, and this continues until you come to

The Cobb, Lyme Regis. (Walk 1).

West Bay harbour. (Walks 14 and 15).

The ancient ridgeway, looking west from Thorncombe Beacon.
(Walks 12 and 14).

Mapperton Manor House. (Walk 19).

Black Ven – another area of massive landslips that is now a nature reserve. Here the cliffs have collapsed and slid right down to the sea's edge, but the slip can be skirted at low tide. Depending on the state of the slip, which is always on the move, there may be a path across its lower end, but this should only be attempted in dry weather.

The blue lias deposits of Black Ven contain the fossilised remains of many weird prehistoric creatures, but it is very dangerous for anyone lacking local knowledge to venture here, because in wet weather there are areas which degenerate into treacherous quagmires.

Beyond Black Ven you have firm sand again, and soon arrive at the mouth of the River Char. Here, in an old stone building, you will find the Charmouth Heritage Coast Centre – open during the summer months and occasionally in winter. It contains interesting displays relating to local wildlife and fossils, and a fascinating collection of old photographs.

In previous editions of this book the next stage of this walk lay along a cliff path that begins immediately W of the Heritage Centre, behind some beach huts. At the time of revising, however, this path has been officially closed due to a landslip. So, instead, your route now lies inland along the road (Lower Sea Lane) that begins just outside the Heritage Centre. After about 300 yards, immediately beyond the primary school, turn left on to a signposted footpath.

This soon brings you on to Higher Sea Lane. Turn right and continue until it brings you out on to the main street in Charmouth. Turn left uphill for a short distance to the shared entry into Old Lyme Road and Old Lyme Hill. The village pound used to be situated in the fork between these two lanes, but the space is now occupied by a very welcome seat.

Take the right-hand fork up Old Lyme Hill, and continue straight on until the lane dwindles to a track that eventually brings you out on to the cliff-top coast path that runs alongside the Lyme Regis golf course. From here one can look down upon the dramatic landslip of Black Ven.

Incidentally, this stretch of cliff-top path is very susceptible to landslips, and many times in the past it has been closed and diversions put in place. Fortunately, *at the time of writing*, it is once again open to the public.

Eventually the golf course is left behind, and the path descends through a fine stand of mature woodland. Soon you emerge on to a track that used to be the road from Lyme Regis to Charmouth, until a long section of it was carried away in a landslip. Turn right past a gate, and continue downhill to the main Lyme Regis road.

Head straight across the road into Colway Lane, directly opposite. This used to be the old mail coach road to Sidmouth and Exeter, but today it sees only local traffic.

After about ½-mile of easy downhill walking you come to Horn Bridge. From here you follow the River Lim back to your starting point at Buddle Bridge, following the waterside footpath to Mill Green; then on downhill via Gosling Bridge, the Lepers' Well and Coombe Street. Details of this route will be found in the opening stages of Walk No. 2.

NOTE: This circular walk can be commenced just as conveniently at Charmouth, using the car park just behind Charmouth beach. It is, of course, vitally important to time your walk so that the shoreline section is traversed on a low, *falling* tide.

19

Points of Interest

Fossils. The stretch of coast between Lyme and Charmouth is famous for its fossils of creatures which flourished between 195 and 150 million years ago, during the Jurassic period. At that stage in our planet's history this part of West Dorset was still being formed beneath an ancient sea inhabited by weird-looking shellfish and reptiles.

Two kinds of fossil are very abundant in the liassic deposits which were laid down upon the bed of this sea. They are the pencil-shaped belemnites, and the beautifully coiled and ribbed ammonites. The latter, which vary greatly in size, were distant ancestors of our present-day nautilus — although Hutchins, in his monumental history of Dorset written some 200 years ago, declared them to be the petrified tails of sea-horses!

Above all, however, the Jurassic period was the age of reptiles, and the diligent fossil hunter may also chance upon their remains among the blue lias beds. Undoubtedly the most famous pioneer of fossil hunting was Mary Anning, the daughter of a curiosity shop keeper in Lyme Regis. In 1811, when still a ten year old schoolgirl, she chanced upon the fossilised remains of a giant icthyosaurus — a kind of porpoise-shaped marine reptile. The fossilised skeleton was 25 feet in length, and it was the first of its kind known to science. Young Mary spent ten years chiselling the monster from its rocky tomb, and at the end of all that patient labour she was paid £23 for it. It eventually became an exhibit in the British Museum.

Mary Anning went on to make fossil-hunting her life's work, but although she achieved international fame with her discoveries she certainly never made a fortune. In more recent times, however, good quality fossils have acquired a considerable value.

Walk No. 5
Wootton Hill Forest Trail

Distance: 1¼ miles.
O.S. Map: SY 29/39 (1:25000) or 193 (1:50000)

THE Forestry Commission have provided a car parking space among the trees for motorists wishing to make this very enjoyable and interesting walk. They have even provided some rustic tables and benches in case you wish to have a picnic.

All they ask in return is that you take great care not to cause a fire, and do not leave any litter. Also, if you have children, you should warn them against climbing or sitting on stacked timber, as this can cause accidents.

It is possible that some of you may consider a 1¼ mile walk to be too short to merit attention. However, the distance can be increased by combining this walk with Walk No. 6 — the same car parking area being ideally situated for both routes.

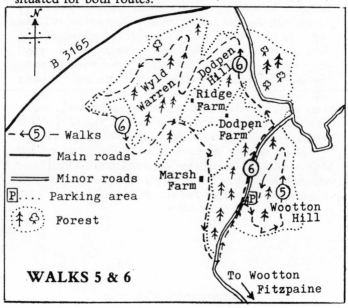

WALKS 5 & 6

The parking area is about 1½ miles NW of Wootton Fitzpaine village. To reach it, leave Wootton Fitzpaine by the Monkton Wyld road. Fork right after about ½ mile; then fork left shortly afterwards at a signpost which reads: "Lambert's Castle and Forest Trail".

The Wootton Hill plantations are a comparatively small part of Charmouth Forest, which covers a total area of approximately 1,200 acres. Due to the thin soil, most of the trees in the Wootton Hill section are of coniferous species, with some beech, sycamore and a few naturally reinstated birch, rowan and ash. This pleasant mixture of deciduous and coniferous trees provides an ideal habitat for a wide variety of birds, whilst mammals include foxes, badgers and roe deer.

However, what makes this forest trail particularly interesting is the fact that, in a comparatively small area, one can study and compare the "recognition features" of a wide variety of coniferous species, including Scots Pine, Corsican Pine, Monterey Pine, Douglas Fir, European Larch and Sitka Spruce, to name just a few.

This nature trail is along fairly level forest roads and tracks, and for this reason it is specially recommended for elderly walkers who can no longer cope with Dorset's more hilly terrain as easily as they used to.

Walk No. 6

Another Forest Walk

Forest Trail Car Park — Dodpen Hill — Wyld Warren
— Marsh Farm — Forest Trail Car Park
Distance: Approx. 5 miles.
O.S. Map: SY 29/39 (1:25000) or 193 (1:50000)

THIS walk definitely comes into the Five Star category! It is a delight at any time of the year, mid-winter included, but is possibly at its best in the spring when wild flowers are plentiful and the woods are echoing to the sound of birdsong.

On leaving the car parking area, turn right along the tarred Council road, passing on your left an unsurfaced forestry road which joins the tarred road at an acute angle. About 200 yards beyond this spot, turn down the forestry road on the left, signposted Dodpen Farm. Then fork right after about 100 yards on to a lesser-used track which will take you in a NW direction for about ¼ mile. After that your route crosses another track, and then bears almost due N for a while before circling around the wooded slopes of Dodpen Hill. Eventually you will join up with another forest road which runs downhill through the trees in an almost straight line.

Turn left down this for about ¼ mile until you come to another forest road branching off to your right. Take this right turning, and you will now be on a very pleasant contour track which takes you around the slopes of another forest-covered hill called Wyld Warren.

After about 1¼ miles the track emerges from the trees on to a lane (classified as a bridleway) which runs alongside the NW edge of the forest. Turn left (SE) along the edge of the wood for about 300 yards until you come to a spot where the forest boundary turns sharply NW. Here, a short distance away on your right, you will see a gate leading into a field. Pass through this gate, and then immediately turn left (SE), keeping the field hedge close

23

on your left. The field narrows near the valley bottom, and you will see a gate in a converging hedgerow on your right. Pass through this and turn left (SE) along a grassy track that fords a small stream. The ford is flanked by a small footbridge that has been thoughtfully covered with a non-slip mat of wire netting.

Your route now passes through a gate into a pasture field. Staying in the same field, turn right past a small barn. Keeping the hedge on your right (E curving to NE), head towards the edge of the nearby forest, where a gate gives access to a grassy bridleway through the trees.

Continue NW along this track for about ¼-mile until you come to a small waymark post indicating a footpath branching off to the right (E) away from the main forestry roads. Head down this path, which begins as a downhill track bordered by over-arching trees, but soon narrows to a path flanked by bracken and brambles.

Soon the path brings you out on to an overgrown forest track. Go straight across this track and pass through a waymarked gate leading into a pasture field. Head SSE towards the bottom of the field. This will bring you to a stile where you can cross a stripling tributary of the River Char.

Still heading SE, you now climb the other side of the valley towards a field gate that leads on to a bridleway. Turn right (S) along this lane, and continue past Marsh Farm until you come to a tarred by-road. Turn left along this road and it will soon bring you back to the forest car park.

Walk No. 7

A Tributary of the Char

Charmouth — Wootton Fitzpaine — Conegar Hill —
Catherston Manor — Charmouth
Distance: Approx. 5½ miles (or 6½ miles if starting and
ending at Charmouth beach car park).
O.S. Map: SY 29/39 (1:25000) or 193 (1:50000)

ALTHOUGH visiting motorists will probably
commence this walk at the car park just behind
Charmouth beach, your escape into the countryside really
begins near the traffic lights in the centre of the village.
From here you walk up Barr's Lane, which leads past the
village playing fields and then dwindles to a public
footpath. Very soon, after crossing some grassland, this
path burrows beneath the new Charmouth by-pass by

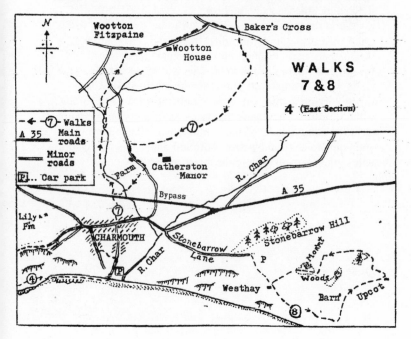

way of an underpass. Emerging at the other side, head on up a slight rise, and then bear away very slightly to your right, aiming for the bottom of the valley. This brings you to a pleasant little tributary of the River Char.

For the next half-mile or so the right-of-way keeps close to the W bank of the stream, diverging only to skirt the edge of a small spinney. Eventually, where there is a sharp double bend in the stream, you come to a footbridge, and here your path crosses to the E bank. After continuing along this bank for a little way you will come to a shallow ford. There's a small footbridge alongside the fording place, but it is craftily hidden behind some bushes and when I travelled this way I only noticed the bridge after wading through the water!

From here you should head approximately N across a grassy field towards a white wicket gate set in a hedge. This in turn gives access to a track which brings you out on to a minor road close to Wootton Fitzpaine. This tiny village derives its name from the Fitzpaine family, who were lords of the manor here as long ago as the reign of Edward II.

The right-of-way continues through a gate on the opposite side of the road. If you head for a waymarked power pole in the middle of the field, and then on to the stream beyond, you'll come to another footbridge. The waymarked path continues roughly NE, and then E, until a stile brings you out just W. of Wootton House — an impressive mansion dating from the 1700's. It is recorded that one of its early owners — a certain Mr. Rose — died in great agony on the 17th January, 1747, and was found to have a stone in his kidney weighing 8oz. 1 dram!

Turn left beyond the stile; then right along the nearby public road — soon passing the little church which stands right alongside Wootton House. Parts of the church date from Norman times, and it is well worth a visit.

From Wootton continue along the lane leading to Whitchurch Canonicorum for about ½ mile until you come to a road junction with the name "Baker's Cross" on top of its signpost. About ten yards W of this signpost you'll see a footpath rising steeply up the roadside bank. This path is easily missed unless you know where to look, because it is almost hidden behind a thicket of small roadside shrubs.

Follow this path (actually it is classified as a bridleway) and it will lead you along the edge of a field into a beautiful wood of mixed beech, larch and pines. The trees extend upwards to the summit of Conegar Hill, and on emerging from the far side of the wood your path will lead you S towards a field gate.

Pass through this gate, and also through another directly facing it on the opposite side of a rough cart track. The bridleway now runs roughly SW, keeping to the high ground, and providing grand views over the Marshwood Vale and across Wootton Fitzpaine towards Lamberts Castle and the Monkton Wyld country.

After skirting another spinney, and passing through a small hillside wood of beech trees, you come eventually to a rough lane which before long brings you out on to a tarred minor road.

Turn left along this road, and after about 300 yards you'll arrive at the imposing entrance gates to Catherston Manor. Immediately opposite there is a signposted gate in the hedge bordering the lane. This leads into a grassy field, and from here you head downhill into the valley bottom, where you will come once more to the tunnel under the Charmouth by-pass. Turn left through this underpass, and head back along the path you followed in the early stages of your walk. This will soon bring you back to your starting point in the centre of Charmouth.

Points of Interest

Village Pound. Shortly after passing Wootton Fitzpaine church, look out for a small walled enclosure alongside a farm entrance. This is the "pound", in which stray or trespassing cattle were impounded until any damage done by them had been paid for by the owner.

Walk No. 8
Stonebarrow Hill, Charmouth

Distance: Approx. 3½ miles.
O.S. Map: SY 29/39 (1:25000) or 193 (1:50000)

THIS walk embraces the eastern end of the National Trust's Golden Cap Estate, and offers outstanding views of the local countryside and coastline. To reach the National Trust car park, where your walk begins, first drive along the A35 to the E outskirts of Charmouth. Just E of the 'Jet' filling station you turn off up a steep, narrow tarred lane. After ¾ mile the lane crosses a cattle grid and promptly degenerates into a rough track. At the same time it brings you on to a grand expanse of open countryside — a patchwork of sheep-nibbled turf and golden-flowering gorse bushes.

You can park your car beside the track, and at the W end of this parking area you'll see a signpost marked "Bridleway" pointing S down the hillside. Follow the path it indicates until you come to a second "Bridleway" signpost pointing to your left. IGNORE this sign and continue straight on downhill until your path joins up with a gated farm track. Bear right down this track, passing through the gate, until you come to lonely Westhay Farm — now converted by the National Trust into two holiday flats. Here the lane ends, and is replaced by a path which takes you across a pleasant expanse of semi-wild pastureland to the cliff-edge.

For a while the path more or less follows the line of the cliffs, but then curves inland to avoid a series of landslips. This diversion takes you in a NE direction across more grassy fields to join up with an unsurfaced cart track near Upcot Farm. Turn left on to this track and follow it until it peters out alongside a small wood.

From the N tip of this wood a field path runs almost due W, passing just N of another wood of mixed beech, ash and pines. A small and rather sad monument, half-hidden in the shadow of the trees, bears the following inscription: "This stone marks the spot where Robert Henry Hilyard fell dead whilst out shooting September

28

6th 1876, aged 40. He was second secretary in H.M. Diplomatic Service, Lord of the Manor of Catherston and J.P. for the County. He was the only child of his mother, and she was a widow."

A spring rises a little distance away at the top end of the wood, and the sound of its waters hurrying downhill among the trees mingles pleasantly with the sound of birdsong and wind-rustled leaves.

A footpath runs through this wood, and the easiest way to locate it is to follow the boundary fence around until you come to a stile near the SE corner. There is a similar stile in the W boundary fence.

After emerging from the far side of the wood your path continues westwards, and soon brings you back on to the track leading to Westhay Farm. Turn right up this track and return to the car parking area by the same path that you followed when setting out.

NOTE: Non-motorists and others wishing to start this walk from Charmouth, instead of driving a car to the top of Stonebarrow Hill, should take the cliff path which begins just E of the river mouth. This is a pleasanter (and safer!) route for the pedestrian than narrow Stonebarrow Lane.

Walk No. 9

Seatown and Golden Cap

Distances: Route (i) 3 miles; (ii) 3½ miles; (iii) 4½ miles.
O.S. Map: SY 49/59 (1:25000) or 193 (1:50000)

THE tiny hamlet of Seatown consists only of a pub
(the Anchor Inn), a disused watermill, and about half-a-

WALKS
9, 10, 11, 12, & 13

- ←⑩- - Walks
──── Main roads
═══ Minor roads
🅿 ..... Parking area
Forest

dozen houses and cottages. Situated in the mouth of a valley, with rolling turf-covered downs on either side, the settlement is dwarfed by the 626 ft. high headland of Golden Cap, which rises abruptly from the end of the shingle beach about ¾ mile to the west. It is the highest point on the south coast of England, and derives its name from the upper layer of yellow sandstone which glows with a rich golden hue when the sun shines upon it. By way of contrast, the lower slopes of the headland are draped with fossil-bearing strata of sombre grey-blue lias.

The walk from Seatown to the summit of Golden Cap is one of the most popular in all Dorset. Taken steadily, it is not particularly arduous — although it does help if one is reasonably sound in wind and limb!

The most important thing, however, is to choose a fine day with good visibility, because the view from the top is really outstanding.

If starting your walk from Seatown car park you should first make your way to the W side of the river mouth. Here, a few yards seaward of the Anchor Inn, you'll see a signpost indicating a footpath which starts off along a stretch of low, hummocky undercliff land for about 100 yards; then bears away to the right and climbs up to the cliff-top proper.

From here all the land you see ahead of you forms part of the National Trust's Golden Cap Estate, which in total includes some 1676 acres of hill, cliff, farmland, undercliff and beach, extending along about five miles of coast between Charmouth and Eype's Mouth. As usual, the National Trust have been lavish with their waymarks and signposts, and a clearly defined footpath leads you steadily upwards, keeping fairly close to the cliff-edge for much of the way.

Peering over the cliff-edge you look down upon a tumbled expanse of landslips swathed in a dense undergrowth of bracken, gorse, brambles and small, gale-stunted trees. This "useless" undercliff area makes an excellent unofficial nature reserve, and is the haunt of many wild creatures, including foxes, badgers, fallow deer and fugitive pheasants.

Incidentally, these undercliff landslips are forever on the move, with fresh falls from above taking the place of material eroded at beach level by stormy seas. The coastline hereabouts recedes on average by about 3 ft. a year, and it is interesting to note that in 1880 there were still many older inhabitants of the village who remembered a farmhouse and barton (rickyard) on the seaward side of the Anchor Inn, on the site of the present beach, and beyond that a road leading to Golden Cap.

It is also recorded that in November 1824 several houses at Seatown were destroyed during a terrible gale which drove the sea to an unprecedented height.

With these snippets of local history to occupy our thoughts, we soon arrive at the base of the Cap itself, where the smooth sheep-nibbled turf gives way to thick heather. The old path to the summit used to go straight up the E side of the Cap, but a few years ago it had become so eroded by countless thousands of scrabbling boots that the National Trust made a replacement path on the inland side — at the same time adding a few "zig-zags" to make the gradient a bit easier.

Although not visible from below, there is an extensive area of relatively level ground on top of Golden Cap, and after arriving at the summit it is well worth walking to the W end of this "plateau" overlooking the St. Gabriel's valley. It is at this end that one also obtains a spectacular gull's-eye view of the golden cliff-face, which at one point is sharply ridged, like the spine of some prehistoric monster. During the Second World War this *very* crumbly ridge was used to train specially selected cliff-climbing Commando units. They used to make some of their ascents in total darkness!

If the tide is low you will also be able to look down upon the complex reef which stretches out to sea from the base of the cliffs. Notice how, in some places, the huge boulders are neatly arranged in semi-circles to form natural rock pools. The largest and most perfectly formed of these lagoons is known locally as the "Fairy Pool".

This reef, which stretches seawards for nearly a mile beyond the low tide mark, has been formed by the slow erosion of Golden Cap over countless thousands of years — the blue lias and other soft material being washed away to leave the harder rocks lying on the sea-bed.

The semi-circular lagoons, on the other hand, were formed comparitively quickly during long-ago periods of exceptionally wet weather, when "slow-motion avalanches" of semi-liquid blue lias oozed down from the cliffs, pushing hundreds of huge boulders in front of them. Subsequent storms and high tides washed away the mud, leaving the boulders neatly arranged in the way you see them today. The same process, albeit on a much smaller scale, still occurs during prolonged spells of exceptionally wet weather.

Your return to Seatown from the top of Golden Cap can be made by three different routes, depending on the time available and the distance you wish to cover. They are as follows:

(i) The shortest route is to return by the way you came up.

(ii) A slightly longer route is to descend by the path near the Ordnance Survey beacon until it brings you out on to a bridleway just below the heather-covered Cap. You then follow the bridleway in an E direction, aiming for a gate below the SW corner of the dense pine wood covering Langdon Hill. The bridleway then skirts the lower edge of this wood, and you continue to follow it downhill. At two places the track divides, and on each occasion you take the right-hand fork. Eventually you come out on to a by-road. Turn downhill along this road, and after about ¼ mile it brings you back to Seatown.

(iii) Descend from the *western* end of Golden Cap, following the cliff-path for part of the way; then cut across the fields in a NW direction towards the ruins of St. Gabriel's Chapel. (See Walk No. 10). From the old chapel a bridleway heads E around the inland side of Golden Cap, and then curves uphill in a SE direction to bring you to the track below Langdon Woods described in (ii) above. About halfway along the bridleway below Langdon Woods, turn right down a signposted field path which takes you to the cliff path leading back to Seatown.

Walk No. 10
Beachcombing and Fossil Hunting
Seatown — Dead Man's Cove — St. Gabriel's Mouth —
Stanton St. Gabriel — Seatown
Distance: Approx. 4-5 miles.
O.S. Maps: SY 29/39 (1:25000) or 193 (1:50000)

THE outward leg of this walk lies along the foreshore, and for your own safety you are strongly advised to set out from Seatown around low tide — preferably during the last two hours of the ebb, and not later than one hour after dead low water. Also, for reasons which will be explained later, this walk should only be attempted in reasonably dry summer weather, or in winter during a very hard frost.

For visiting motorists there is a car park just behind Seatown beach. From here you set off along the beach towards the foot of Golden Cap, which lies 1 mile to the W. The beach consists mainly of loose shingle, but quite often there is easier walking on firm gritty sand near the low tide line.

On reaching Golden Cap the shingle gives way to a complex reef of tide-exposed boulders, and you will probably be tempted away from your walk for a while to study the fascinating marine life in the rock pools. This reef is a favourite hunting ground for prawning enthusiasts, and on summer days when sea conditions are suitable you will see dozens of them on the outer rocks with their baited drop-nets.

A word of warning, though. Most weed-covered rocks are slippery, but those covered with green silk weed are particularly treacherous — so steer well clear of them if you wish to avoid broken bones!

Another hazard to beware of is the smooth expanse of blue lias bedrock on which many of the boulders are resting. When wet, this rock becomes as slippery as ice.

In many places the surface of this liassic bedrock is sprinkled liberally with fossils, like the currants in a cake. Most plentiful of all are the bullet-shaped inner shells of primitive squid-like creatures called belemnites. More decorative, however, are the whorled and ridged ammonites — the ancestors of our present-day nautilus.

Many of the ammonites found along this stretch of beach are embedded in pieces of glittering, golden-hued iron pyrites. The smaller ones can be about the size of one's finger-nail, and are much sought-after for use in jewellery. Others come much larger; sometimes up to 18 inches in diameter.

After negotiating the main mass of foreshore boulders you will come to another small patch of shingle beach. The set of the inshore currents at this spot causes a wide variety of beachcombing finds to be cast ashore — lobster pot ropes and floats, broken hatch covers, and even the occasional message in a bottle!

In the days of sail, when shipwrecks were all too frequent, the waves also washed in their tragic quota of human flotsam and jetsam, and that's why this patch of beach came to be known as Dead Man's Cove. Inevitably, during the German U-boat campaign of the Second World War, this cove lived up to its name again, but I'll not spoil your walk with gruesome details.

Immediately beyond Dead Man's Cove the crumbling blue lias cliffs rise vertically above the beach. THESE CLIFFS ARE SUBJECT TO FREQUENT FALLS, and on no account should you venture underneath them in your search for fossils. Indeed, this is the main reason why I recommended you to start your walk at low tide. If you keep as close as possible to the low water mark you can pass this danger spot in safety, but even so I don't advise you to linger too long in the vicinity!

From the safety of my boat, while fishing off this stretch of coast, I have witnessed many of these cliff falls, and they really are spectacular. With a roar like thunder a complete slice of the cliff face, several feet thick, collapses in a great cloud of grey dust which can be seen for miles out at sea as it slowly expands and drifts away on the wind.

Heading on along the beach, you now come to a

small, flat-topped promontory which has been formed by a mixture of spring water and semi-liquid blue lias oozing down from the cliffs above. In dry weather it is safe to walk with caution across the top of this promontory, but it is unwise to do so after prolonged rain because the blue lias then turns into a treacherous quagmire.

A few years ago I was dinghy prawning in a nearby cove with a friend when we heard terrified cries for help, and on rowing to investigate we found a young man and his girl-friend already hip-deep in the mud, and still sinking. With the help of our anchor rope we managed, with considerable difficulty, to break the suction and pull them free.

"We were looking for fossils," they explained shakily, when it was all over. "Until you turned up we thought we were going to end up as fossils ourselves!"

Beyond this promontory you come to a long stretch of shingle beach which extends all the way to Charmouth. However, after walking only half a mile along it, you arrive at St. Gabriel's Mouth, where a small stream comes cascading down through a deep gully it has cut in the cliffs.

At this spot the blue lias cliff is low and sloping, and in reasonably dry weather it is a perfectly simple matter to climb up to a grassy path which commences a little way higher up. In winter, however, the blue lias becomes too wet and slippery to provide a safe foothold — the only exception being during periods of very cold weather when the lias is frozen iron hard.

In the days when smuggling was a flourishing profession in West Dorset, this narrow gap in the cliffs was a favourite route for contraband goods.

Shortly after reaching the grassy track above the lias, bear left and cross footbridge to W side of stream; then head directly inland. Soon you will come to a small thatched cottage and a one-time farmhouse that has now been converted by the National Trust into holiday flats. These two dwellings are all that now remains of the "lost" village of Stanton St. Gabriel. This once flourishing little community of fisher and farming folk was deserted centuries ago for reasons which seem to have been forgotten. Nearby is the ruin of St. Gabriel's Chapel — once the village's tiny place of worship. Little remains today except four crumbling walls and a low doorway arch which must have cracked many a long-suffering skull — unless the Dorset folk of yore were a good deal shorter in the shank than they are today!

From the ruined chapel a bridleway runs eastwards around the S edge of St. Gabriel's Wood, and then curves upwards around the lower slopes of Golden Cap to join up with the lane which runs below the S edge of Langdon Hill Woods. About halfway along this edge of the woods you should turn right down a signposted footpath which links up with a cliff path leading back to Seatown.

Points of Interest
St. Gabriel's Chapel. An old photograph, believed to have been taken between 1870-1880, shows this 13th Century chapel complete with a thatched roof that appears to be in quite good condition. Yet by the mid-1930's, when I first knew it, the building had already become a roofless ruin.

A one-time Curate of Chideock, the Rev. T. Worthington, writing in 1880, records that within the memory of his older parishioners, the old chapel of Stanton St. Gabriel had been used as "a receiving house for smuggled kegs". He also tells us that in those days there used to be from thirty to forty fishermen working off Seatown beach — nearly all of them engaged in smuggling, and aided and abetted by the local inhabitants in general.

WARNING! Since the winter of 1989/90 the W. end of Seatown beach has become eroded down to its blue lias bedrock, and around high water the sea now washes right up to the base of the cliffs.

Walk No. 11
Golden Cap — the Easy Way
Langdon Woods — Golden Cap — Langdon Woods
Distance: Approx. 2½ miles.
Forest "contour" walk only — Approx. 1¾ miles.
O.S. Map: SY 49/59 (1:25000) or 193 (1:50000)

THIS very pleasant walk could, I suppose, be called
the "lazy" way of climbing Golden Cap, because one
starts out from the National Trust car park in Langdon
Woods, which is already about 500 ft. above sea level.

To reach this parking area you turn S off the A35 on
to an unsignposted tarred lane situated about 100 yards E
of Frodsham Motors service station, Morcombelake.
Almost immediately after this you turn left on to an
unsurfaced lane, and then after about 300 yards you turn
right up a forest road which ends in the parking area.

From the N and S sides of this car park a circular
forest track sets off around this hill-top expanse of
woodland, which consists mainly of conifers with some
fire-break belts of beech around the perimeter. Local wild
life includes foxes, badgers, grey squirrels, fallow deer
and a wide variety of birds.

This circular forest track is open to walkers, but
padlocked gates at either side of the car park prevent its
use by horses or motor vehicles. Constructed by the
Forestry Commission for occasional use by timber lorries,
the track keeps to the 500 ft. contour line throughout its
length, and therefore offers easy, enjoyable walking for
anyone who, for reasons of age or infirmity, is unable to
manage hills or rough terrain. Gaps in the trees provide
extensive views over the surrounding coast and
countryside, and bench seats beside the track enable one
to enjoy these views in comfort.

The length of this circular walk is about 1¾ miles,
but it can be extended to include a visit to the top of
Golden Cap. Although this optional extension is not
recommended for the very elderly or infirm, it is
nevertheless a lot easier than climbing Golden Cap from
sea level!

For the purpose of these directions, I will assume that you set off along the circular track in a clockwise direction. After walking along the E perimeter of the forest, with its views of Chideock village in the valley below, the track curves around the S end of Langdon Hill. At this point, on your left, you'll see a footpath disappearing downhill into a dense forest of pines. If you wish to climb Golden Cap you should take this side path, which will soon bring you out on to a bridleway at the SW corner of the forest. Turn right and follow the bridleway through a gate into a grassy field. From this point on the path to the top of Golden Cap is clearly waymarked. For further information on Golden Cap, see Walk No. 9.

Your return to Langdon Woods and the circular forest track can be made by the same route. Turn left on re-joining the contour track, and it will eventually complete the circle and bring you back to the car parking area.

Points of Interest

Langdon Hill. The name "Langdon" has Saxon origins, and means "the Long Hill". At one time, prior to tree-planting in the early 1960's, the long, flat summit of this hill was covered with smooth, deer-nibbled turf that was a delight to walk upon. This long "backbone" of Langdon can still be reached from the circular contour track by turning up a side trail on the W side. On reaching the top, if you approach quietly, you are likely to surprise a small herd of grazing deer, or maybe a fox sunning himself on the edge of the undergrowth.

The area on top of the hill now serves as a firebreak, and is therefore kept reasonably clear — although here and there trailing brambles are apt to snag your legs.

At the N end of the hill-top there stands a group of tall pine trees known as "Langdon Clump". Although their numbers have been reduced in recent years through gale damage, the Clump is still a conspicuous landmark for miles around, and is frequently used by local fishermen when taking cross-bearings at sea to pinpoint their fishing grounds.

There is a local belief that the Clump marks the spot where victims of the Great Plague were buried over 300 years ago. If this is true, then the trees must have been replanted many times over, because pines have a comparitively brief life-span.

Walk No. 12
In the Tracks of Prehistoric Man
Seatown — Thorncombe Beacon — Eype Down — Quar
Hill — Chideock — Seatown
Distance: Approx. 5 miles.
O.S. Map: SY 49/59 (1:25000) or 193 (1:50000)

START from the car park situated immediately
behind Seatown beach. Cross the stile at the E side of the
car park, and follow the National Trust cliff path. After
about 300 yards you will have to skirt around the edge of a
large badger sett that has become overgrown with an
impenetrable mass of gorse bushes. (Being nocturnal
creatures, the badgers emerge in the late dusk, and can
often be seen then if you stand quietly on the downwind
side of the sett.)

After climbing steadily for about ¾ mile your route
crosses two stiles set about 100 yards apart. Here a few
words of advice might not come amiss. Many walkers
unfamiliar with the lie of the land make their journey
unnecessarily strenuous by scrambling directly up the
very steep slope of Doghouse Hill.

You will find the going a lot easier if you follow the
prehistoric trackway which skirts the N side of the hill.
This track will lead you up through a small valley on to a
fairly flat expanse of cliff-top, which in turn leads to
another stile just below the 516 ft. summit of Thorncombe
Beacon.

There is a seat on top of the Beacon, so you can sit
and admire the magnificent view in comfort. To the E you
can see the twin piers of Bridport Harbour, with the
wave-pounded Chesil Beach stretching away towards the
distance-hazed promontory of Portland Bill.

Westwards, beyond Golden Cap and Lyme Regis,
the Devon coastline curves around towards Beer Head,
the Exe estuary and Tor Bay, with the high tors of
Dartmoor acting as a backdrop. On a very clear day you
can even see as far as Start Point, some 55 miles distant as
the seagull flies. Unfortunately, when visibility is as good

as this it usually means that heavy rain can be expected within the next 24 hours!

From the top of Thorncombe Beacon the cliff path continues downhill to Eype's Mouth and Bridport Harbour. However, to achieve a circular route (and to avoid losing the height we have so laboriously gained!) we shall continue our walk by heading inland towards a picturesque expanse of bracken-covered common land known as Eype Down.

If you look NE from the summit of Thorncombe Beacon you will see, about 200 yards away, a gorse-grown Ancient British burial mound. Head down towards this tumulus, passing it on your left hand; then climb over a boarded-up gap in the fence which does service for a stile.

Now, keeping to the right-of-way which lies close alongside a hedge, head NE towards a small wood which you'll see about ¼ mile ahead. After skirting the W end of this wood you will find yourself on top of Eype Down. Here the footpath you have been following joins up with a turf-covered bridleway, and this meanders through the bracken and gorse in a more or less northerly direction until it brings you out on to the main Chideock-Bridport road.

Directly opposite, on the other side of the main road, you'll see a narrow lane. Cross the road (take care — the traffic travels fast here and there are blind corners in both directions!) and proceed up this lane. After about 60 yards you will come to a cart track forking off to the left. Take this track, which is a public right-of-way, and after passing through a gate it will lead you up to the top of Quar Hill — this being the old Dorset word for "quarry".

It is difficult to imagine this peaceful hilltop once being a scene of industrial activity, because the steep hollows and mounds of the old quarry workings are now covered with a picturesque mantle of sheep-nibbled turf. Centuries ago the golden-hued stone from these quarries was loaded on to horse-drawn sledges and dragged down the hillside to build the massive walls and towers of now-vanished Chideock castle, and the mellow thatched cottages of the neighbouring village.

The deep grooves in the grassy hillside made by these heavily-laden sledges can still be seen, and if we walk along the hill-top to its W end we can follow one of these old sledge routes (now a right-of-way) down into the bottom of a steep-sided valley. Passing close to a large modern milking parlour and feed barn, our route brings us back to the main A35 road at the E end of Chideock village.

On the opposite side of the road you will see a narrow footpath indicated by a signpost bearing the legend: "TO THE SEA". Follow this path, and after a short distance it will bring you to the banks of the little River Winniford, which has its source a few miles away under the slopes of Hardown Hill.

The path makes a short diversion to skirt the local sewage works; then crosses the river by a bridge and heads diagonally across a caravan site to join Mill Lane. Turn left down this lane, and after passing the old mill house you will quickly return to your starting point in Seatown car park.

This walk is strongly recommended for its magnificent and extensive coastal and inland views. As a winter walk it is particularly impressive when the sun first appears after a heavy fall of snow. At such times the dazzling white cliffs and hills contrast unforgettably with the vivid blue of the sea and sky.

Walk No. 13

A Journey into the "Underworld"

Chideock Manor — North Chideock — Hell Lane —
Henwood Hill — Coppet Hill — North Chideock —
Chideock Manor
Distance: Approx. 5½ miles.
O.S. Maps: SY 49/59 (1:25000) or 193 (1:50000)

MOST of this walk takes you along ancient
packhorse trails and hill-top tracks, with grand views
across the Marshwood Vale towards the Beaminster
Downs, Pilsdon Pen and Lamberts Castle. However,
before we set off I had better warn you that there is one
short stretch of lane down in the valley that runs about an
inch deep in water, summer and winter — so wear a stout
pair of waterproof boots!

Motorists intending to make this walk should first
drive along the A35 to Chideock, and then take the
signposted turning to North Chideock immediately
alongside the village church. After about ¼ mile you will
come to an avenue of trees bordering the grounds of
Chideock Manor. Slow down here and look out for a
sign on your right pointing to the Catholic Church, which
adjoins the manor house. There is plenty of room here to
park your car beside the road, provided you avoid those
times when services are being held in the church.

Begin your walk by continuing N along this quiet
by-road until you come to a "T"-junction, where you
turn right. About 100 yards further on there's a fork in the
road, with a tall pine tree in the middle of the fork. You
turn right here down a one-time packhorse track called
Hell Lane. For a little way the lane boasts a tarred surface,
but after passing an old thatched farmhouse (Hell Farm)
the tarmac ends and for the next 100 yards or so you have
to splash your way through a shallow rivulet of spring
water which runs impetuously downhill among the
tractor ruts and clumps of watercress.

Soon, however, the trail begins to climb steeply around the N flank of Quarry Hill - the haunt of buzzards, kestrels, hares, badgers and foxes.

As the trail nears the crest of the ridge it burrows into a miniature ravine, and from the steep sandstone walls on either side gnarled tree roots protrude like outstretched arms. Walking along this stretch of Hell Lane really is rather like venturing into the Underworld!

Eventually, at a height of nearly 400 ft., the sunken way emerges into daylight to join another ancient trackway which runs along the "backbone" of this short range of uplands. Turn left at this junction, and continue to follow the old track until an overgrown and blocked-off section compels you to continue your journey on the grassy hillside bordering the old way.

Heading roughly NW, you skirt the SW slopes of Denhay Hill. The right of way then heads roughly W along the line of a hedgerow, passing close on your right to an O.S. trig beacon on the E flank of Coppet Hill. It is worth making the short diversion to this beacon in order to admire the magnificent view of the Marshwood Vale directly below, with the prehistoric hillforts of Lambert's Castle, Pilsdon Pen and Lewesdon rising beyond.

From the trig beacon you now head due W towards a gate which lies hidden from sight over the brow of the hill. Pass through this gate, and then through another one close by, and follow the hedgeline on your left. This hedge curves around gently until it is heading approximately WSW, with Charmouth and Lyme Regis visible above the top of the hedge.

Shortly after this the hedge curves around quite abruptly to the right and heads roughly NNW. At this stage many walkers begin to think that they are heading in completely the wrong direction for their return route, and try to take a short cut through the first available gap in the hedge. Don't make this mistake, but carry on for another 200 yards or so until you come to a stile set in the hedge. Cross this stile, but take care because it is immediately followed by a steep earthy slope which becomes very slippery after rain.

After descending this slope on whichever part of your anatomy happens to be most convenient, you follow the hedge on your left down to the bottom of a grassy field. Here you turn left through an iron gate bearing a blue bridleway arrow, and head S into a pleasant grassy coombe. This trail you are now following is an ancient one, and was almost certainly trodden by the inhabitants of the Iron Age hillforts of Pilsdon and Lewesdon on their visits to the coast - perhaps to barter for fish. Later it was used by generations of cattle drovers. It must also have seen many nocturnal journeyings by smugglers' contact men transporting contraband inland from Seatown - once notorious for its free-trading activities.

After passing through another waymarked gate you continue roughly S, keeping as close as possible to the treeline on your right. Before long another waymarked gate leads you back on to the old track. It is interesting to see how, over the centuries, the plodding hooves of all those passing beasts have worn it into a "hollow-way" in the hillside that is over 10 feet deep in places.

Eventually the track brings you out on to a tarred lane. Continue straight on (S) along this lane for about ½-mile until you come to a T-junction. Turn left here, and then after only 50 yards or so turn right. This brings you back on to the lane you set out along, and very soon you will find yourself back at the parked car.

Walk No. 14
West Bay to Thorncombe Beacon
West Bay — Eype's Mouth — Thorncombe Beacon —
Lower Eype — West Bay
Distance: Approx. 6 miles.
O.S. Maps: SY 49/59 (1:25000) or 193 (1:50000)

THIS very enjoyable walk, with its wonderful coastal and inland views, is a favourite with holiday visitors staying in the Bridport/West Bay area. It is worth mentioning, however, that the circular route can be started and ended just as conveniently at Eype's Mouth car park, or from the lay-by on Eype Down. (See Note 1).

Walkers starting from West Bay harbour should head W along the sea front until, at the end of the promenade, they see the cliff path rising directly ahead. After following the path over some hilly pastureland, flanked on its seaward side by an area of tumbled landslips, you begin the descent to Eype's Mouth. Here a

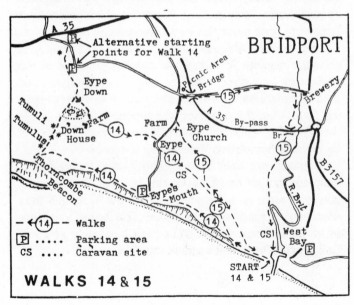

small stream trickles out of a deep coombe on to a pleasant beach of mixed shingle and coarse, gritty sand. The village of Eype lies about ½ mile inland, within the sheltering embrace of the coombe.

You pick up the cliff path again by the car park on the far side of the valley, and you now begin the climb of Thorncombe Beacon, whose golden-hued cliffs dominate the skyline about a mile ahead. With a height of 515 ft., it is the second highest point on the south coast — Golden Cap, a couple of miles further west, topping it by just over 100 ft.

The path is clearly defined, and for the first ¾ mile it keeps fairly close to the cliff-edge. After that, however, your easiest route curves inland a little way to circle around the rim of a huge amphitheatre-shaped hollow, over 200 ft. deep. Near the bottom of this hollow there is a spring which almost certainly provided water for the prehistoric tribesmen who once lived on these uplands. From weather-eroded sections of these local cliffs I have retrieved dozens of flint scrapers and arrowheads.

On a clear day you will be rewarded with a magnificent view from the summit of Thorncombe Beacon, and the main landmarks to look for are mentioned in Walk No. 12.

You begin the next stage of your walk by heading inland towards an Ancient British burial mound, situated 100 yards NNE of the seat on top of the Beacon. Pass this tumulus on your left hand, and then, after climbing over a nearby stile, continue NNE alongside a hedge towards a small wood which you'll see directly ahead of you.

Another stile leads on to Eype common. Head up a short slope; then turn right downhill along a winding track. Turn right again towards the lower end of the wood.

At the E end of the wood the footpath brings you out near some farm buildings. If you look towards the E corner of these buildings you will see a modified form of "squeezer stile", shaped like a narrow doorframe. Your right-of-way passes through this stile, then heads SE across grassy fields towards Eype village, which is visible about a mile distant. After passing through two more stiles, both of them waymarked with arrows, you should bear away almost due E. This will take you downhill to a small gate that is half-hidden in the corner of a hedge.

After passing through this gate you will see a rough track directly ahead. Follow this downhill, and very soon you'll come to a series of "Footpath" direction signs which will guide you around some cow sheds and silage clamps, and through two large iron gates, on to a concrete road. Turn right when the concrete gives way to a tarred surface, and then left, and soon you'll find yourself in the middle of Lower Eype village.

Turn right down the village street; then left past a cottage called "Pilgrim's Latch". Directly facing you, at the next corner of the road, you'll see a gate giving access to a grassy field. A public right-of-way runs SE across this field, and you should follow this by keeping close to the hedge on your right-hand side. After 230 yards you will come to a stile, and here your path crosses to the other side of the hedge; then takes you across a caravan site before returning to open fields.

On emerging from the caravan site you are rewarded with a fine view of West Bay harbour. By heading directly towards Pier Terrace (this is a prominent block of flats overlooking the harbour basin), you will soon come to another stile near the far corner of the field.

Your path now runs close alongside a hedge on your left-hand side, and through gaps in this hedge you will see an ancient packhorse trail running parallel with your path. It is worth bearing this track in mind, because it offers interesting possibilities for a future walk. (See Walk No. 15).

Very soon your path brings you out into the NW outskirts of West Bay, and another ½ mile of easy downhill walking brings you back to the sea front promenade and your starting point near the harbour.

NOTE 1. Motorists wishing to commence this walk from Eype Down should turn off the A35 at the top of Furchase Hill (1 mile E of Chideock). About 600 yards beyond this turn-off point there is limited grass verge parking, and from here a path heads uphill through the bracken to the crest of the hill. A grassy track meanders in a S to SE direction along the crest of the hill, and after about ½-mile connects with the circular route of this walk at the W end of the small wood beside Down House.

NOTE 2. I would strongly advise motorists NOT to re-enter the A35 by the Furchase Hill junction mentioned above. This can be a very dangerous spot for emerging traffic, with fast-moving vehicles approaching round a completely blind bend. A much safer exit route would be to carry on along the picturesque Eype Down road for a mile. Bearing left at the next road junction, this takes you past the picnic area mentioned in NOTE 3, and out on to the A35.

NOTE 3. The signposted picnic area adjoining the Bridport by-pass (A35) also makes a good alternative starting point for this walk. From the picnic area head S down the lane leading to Lower Eype village. From here you follow the walk directions, commencing at the second paragraph on page 49.

Walk No. 15

By Packhorse Trail to Eype

West Bay — Eype Church — Brewery Hill — West Bay
Distance: Approx. 4 miles.
O.S. Maps: SY 49/59 (1:25000) or 193 (1:50000)

THIS walk explores the old packhorse trail that we glimpsed during the final stages of Walk No. 14. Starting from West Bay harbour, you head W along the sea front and then climb the path which runs between the cliff-edge and the houses.

After passing the last house, and entering the open field beyond, you veer away from the cliff-edge and head diagonally across the field towards its NW corner. Here you pass through a gate between the field hedge and the garden of a bungalow. Just beyond this gateway, on your left, you will see the start of the bridleway, which is barely an arm's span in width, and tunnels intriguingly between high stone-reinforced banks and over-arching hedges of rampant blackthorns.

The old trail is easy to follow until it suddenly brings you out on to a grassy hilltop crowned by a tall T.V. booster mast. At this point the track divides, with a pedestrian right-of-way forking off to the right in the direction of Watton House Farm, while your route along the bridleway continues straight ahead, passing close under the left-hand side of the T.V. mast.

Pause for a few moments on this hill-top to admire the grand view of Bridport, set against a backcloth of rolling green hills. Notice how lots of these hills are terraced with strip lynchets — the result of primitive farming techniques of bygone times.

About 100 yards beyond the T.V. mast you pass through a white-painted gate, and once more your route is clearly defined. You pass straight across a tarred lane, picking up the old packhorse trail again on the opposite side, and soon this brings you out on to another tarred lane beside Eype Church — which stands on a hill-top high above the village itself.

51

From where the bridleway emerges on to the tarred lane, a public right-of-way heads NE across a field for about 150 yards, and then meets up with another tarred lane. Turn right along this lane, and follow it down a steep hill (known locally as Brewery Hill or Skilling Hill) into the valley of the River Brit.

Beside the river, in a pleasant aroma of hops, stands an unusual thatched brewery equipped with a waterwheel — the home of Palmer's Beers. Just before you reach the brewery you will see a path leading off to your right along the river bank. If you follow this it will take you very pleasantly across flat green meadows to the caravan site at West Bay. A continuation of this public right-of-way runs along the E side of the caravan site, and this soon brings you back to the harbour at West Bay.

NOTE 1: An alternative return route to West Bay would be to turn downhill at Eype Church, passing through Eype village to Eype's Mouth, and from there over the cliffs to West Bay.

NOTE 2: The Bridport by-pass, opened in 1988, now crosses the final stage of this walk by a flyover bridge. The footpath passes beneath the bridge, and remains as pleasant as ever.

Walk No. 16

Grand Views and Lonely Turf Tracks

Burton Bradstock — Bredy North Hill — Hammiton Hill
— Shipton Hill — Shipton Gorge — Burton Bradstock
Distance: Approx. 7 miles.
O.S. Maps: SY 49/59 (1:25000) or 194 (1:50000)

MOTORISTS visiting Burton Bradstock to sample
this very enjoyable walk will probably find a parking
space outside the church, in Church Street. However, on
days when a service is due to be held in the church, it
would be a matter of courtesy to park elsewhere. Annings
Lane is a convenient alternative, because from here a
public footpath leads down to the first leg of our walk
alongside the River Bride. (The path from Annings Lane
commences directly opposite a cul-de-sac clearly marked
"Norburton").

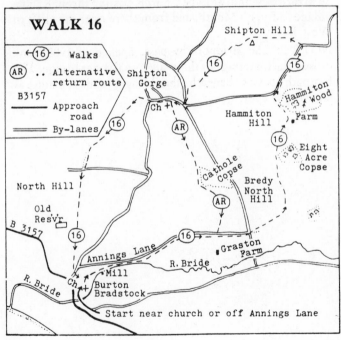

Unstable cliffs between Dead Man's Cove and St. Gabriel's Mouth. For cautionary remarks, see Walk 10.

Low tide rock pools, viewed from the summit of Golden Cap. (Walks 9, 10, and 11).

The bridleway and lake, looking north towards Hooke Park Forest.
(Walks 18 and 19).

Seatown Beach, looking west towards Golden Cap.
(Walks 9, 10 and 11).

If you park by the church, you should first walk down Darby Lane, and then turn right into Grove Road. Look out for Grove House, on your left, which has a magnificent old mulberry tree in the front garden, its branches supported on crutches.

Soon the road ends near a picturesque watermill, and you now follow a riverside path until it bears away to the left and brings you out on to a tarred lane.

Continue E along this lane for about ¾ mile until you come to a large concrete silage clamp built immediately alongside a crossways. Proceed straight across this junction on to a farm track. After 300 yards you'll come to a gate on your left leading into a grassy field, with a leaning fence post alongside the gate forming a squeeze stile. Pass through this stile; turn right; pass through another gate; then turn left and head N over the grassy flank of Bredy North Hill.

From the crest of this hill you continue N, skirting the W edge of a small wood called Eight Acre Copse. You now begin to climb again around the dramatically contoured E flank of Hammiton Hill.

On the far side of this hill the bridleway joins up with a farm track, and you turn left along this for about 200 yards until it emerges on to a tarred but very pleasant by-road. Turn right along this road. After just over ¼ mile you will see a signpost on your left indicating a bridleway to Higher Sturthill and Vinney Cross. I suggest you pass this by, and instead take the signposted footpath which commences about 100 yards further on along the road.

This path climbs very pleasantly along the crest of a grassy ridge towards the summit of Shipton Hill — one of West Dorset's many Iron Age hill-forts. Nearly 560 ft. high, and surrounded by a single turf-covered rampart, the appearance of this hill varies according to one's viewpoint. From out at sea it looks like a huge cone with the top cut off, and this very distinctive shape makes it a useful navigational landmark for mariners and fishermen.

The footpath follows the line of the old rampart around the S slope of Shipton Hill, but having climbed this far I would strongly recommend you to continue right to the top, and then walk the length of the level grassy summit. You will be rewarded with grand views in all directions, and in autumn you may also find some wild mushrooms.

At the W end of the hill a prehistoric turf causeway leads you down to rejoin the footpath, which now leads almost due SW towards the very picturesque village of Shipton Gorge, with its ancient church, sited on a steep knoll, standing guard over the cottages below.

You head W straight through the village street until you come to a cross-roads — the "road" heading W on the far side of the junction being a rough unsurfaced lane. Continue along this lane for about 100 yards, then pass through a field gate on your left. A right-of-way runs SW across this field, and if you keep fairly close to the left-hand hedge you will arrive at a stile set in a gap in the hedge. (See NOTE 1). From here the path continues SW across four more fields and stiles, and then emerges on to a farm track. Turn left along this track for 100 yards until, almost directly opposite a sharp left-hand bend, you will see a field gate marked with a blue bridlepath waymark.

Pass through this gate and head due S. This will take you very pleasantly across the crest of North Hill, past a disused and overgrown reservoir (where in spring I have on several occasions seen a vixen with her cubs), and so down a rather overgrown green lane which emerges beside Shadrach Farm, on the outskirts of Burton Bradstock. From here it is only a few minutes' walk back to your parked car.

NOTE 1: This stile is in a rather dilapidated condition at the time of writing, but it can be negotiated quite easily.

NOTE 2: There is an alternative return route from Shipton Gorge to Burton Bradstock. From the centre of Shipton village a public footpath runs up alongside the church; then heads SSE down the valley of a small stream, skirting the W side of Cathole Copse before emerging on to a tarred lane opposite Graston Farm entrance. Turn right along this lane for Burton Bradstock.

Walk No. 17

A Journey into the Past

Eggardon Hill — King's Farm — Whetley — Powerstock
Forest — Eggardon Hill
Distance: Approx. 6 - 7 miles.
O.S. Maps: SY 49/59 (1:25000) or 194 (1:50000)

THIS super walk offers us a glimpse of Dorset as it must have been long ago, in the days before history began. It covers some lonely countryside in the "back of beyond" so we must use a car to reach our starting point near the ancient hill fort on top of Eggardon Hill.

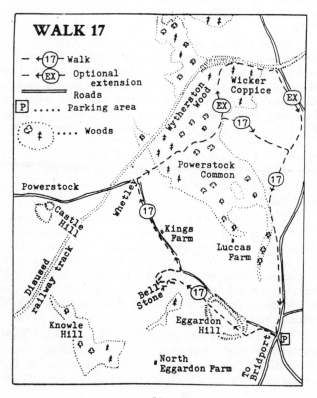

The easiest way to approach Eggardon is along the narrow and little-used Roman road which loops northwards from the modern A35 between Vinney Cross (2½ miles E of Bridport) and the foot of Lambert's Hill (¾ mile E of Winterborne Abbas).

If approaching from Vinney Cross, your road soon climbs up along an old smugglers' route known as the Spyway, where the present-day traveller can refresh himself at the very pleasant 17th Century Spyway Inn.

About 1½ miles beyond the Spyway Inn you will notice a triangulation beacon close to the road, and some 100 yards past this point you will come to a cross-roads. If you turn right here and stop immediately after doing so, you will find plenty of space to park your car on the wide verge.

After parking the car, head straight back over the cross-roads on to a rough lane signposted: "Powerstock — Unfit for Cars". After only 100 yards you quit the lane through a gate on the left, which gives access on to a bridleway. Head SW across the turf and soon, on breasting a rise, you will arrive at the E entrance of the hill fort. Here, after climbing over a stile, you follow a footpath which crosses three mighty turf-covered ramparts, and then strides in a NW direction across the top of this huge stronghold, which was inhabited over a very long period of time that embraced both the Bronze Age and the Iron Age.

The thing which must surely impress everyone who visits this spot is the incredible amount of labour which went into the raising of these earthworks. Each of the ramparts is about 30 ft. high from ditch to crest, and they encompass some twenty acres. It was a fantastic feat, bearing in mind the primitive tools used, and the fact that every spadeful of earth was carried up the steep banks in wicker baskets.

The fact that this mammoth task was successfully completed after centuries of work, involving many generations, says a lot for the determination and organisation of the one-time inhabitants of this hill-top.

They must also have been a pretty hardy lot, because the camp stands over 800 ft. above sea level, and in winter the wind up here has an edge to it like a butcher's knife.

After travelling the full length of the hill fort, the footpath emerges from the ramparts again and continues along the crest of a steep-sided spur of the hill. After a while you come to a spot where a combination of erosion and landslips have exposed a steep, rocky escarpment, and at the foot of this you will see a hoary, weather-worn boulder standing amongst the bracken and brambles. This is the Bell Stone, and tradition has it that it featured in the religious rites of the ancient tribesmen who lived on Eggardon. If there's any truth in this, then the shelf-like rock escarpment would have provided them with an excellent vantage point from which to view the proceedings.

Several other large boulders — moss-covered and therefore not so conspicuous — are arranged around the Bell Stone in a rough semi-circle; whilst a little further W, and hidden from view under a thicket of elders and blackthorns, there is a crude "circle" of five stones.

There is no doubt that all these boulders originally tumbled down from the escarpment above, probably as a result of natural erosion. Nevertheless, the fact that several of them are standing upright, and not recumbent, would seem to indicate that some, at least, were deliberately man-handled into their present positions.

A short distance away, on either side of the near-precipitous escarpment, it is possible to pick one's way quite safely down a tussocky hillside to the Bell Stone. From here your easiest route would be to continue W around the foot of the hillside for about 100 - 150 yards, until you come to a rough track leading up over the top of the spur — which at this point is considerably reduced in height. The track, made by a family of badgers, leads past the entrance to their sett, which burrows under crevices in the hillside rock strata. The last time I passed this way, on a day in late February, the badgers were already busy with their spring cleaning, and throwing out their old winter bedding of dead bracken and grass.

The track continues over the top of the spur, which is knife-edged at this point, and then makes a scrambling but safe descent down the other side. From here you head NE across a boulder-littered area of scrub and grass until you encounter a rough cart track. Turn right along this, and then left when you come to a tarred lane. This narrow and very picturesque by-way takes you downhill past King's Farm to the little hamlet of Whetley.

Just beyond Whetley Farm, which lies at the foot of the stream-threaded valley, you will see on your right a triangular patch of grass with some apple trees growing on it. On the far (W) side of this is a signpost marked: "Bridleway to Stones Common". Turn right along this track, and it will take you in a NE direction across some grassy fields and a plantation of young conifers. After that it enters the ancient forest of Powerstock Common. Parts of this woodland are hazel coppice, which have become rather neglected since wattle sheep hurdles went out of fashion. For the most part, however, the trees consist mainly of mature oaks and ash, and this part of the forest can have changed very little since it was hunted by King Athelstan over a thousand years ago.

Tradition has it that this grandson of King Alfred built a hunting palace on a nearby hill overlooking the village of Powerstock. It is certainly true that, later on, the Normans built a castle on the same spot. Sadly the old castle no longer exists, but the turf-covered motte and bailey can still be seen.

Descendants of the deer that Athelstan once hunted are still plentiful in the forest, and you stand a good chance of seeing some of them if you walk quietly. Dogs, of course, should be kept on a lead — especially when the does are in fawn or nursing their young.

The bridleway climbs steadily uphill and emerges on the far side of the forest. (See Note 1). Here you should follow another bridleway that sets off in an ESE direction, and brings you to Barrowland Farm after about

¾ mile. At the farm itself you now turn right and head SSW along a bridleway that eventually brings you out on to the old Roman road. Turn right (S) along this, and after less than ¾ mile you will arrive back at your parked car.

NOTE 1: If you prefer, the forest walk can be extended as follows: Instead of emerging from the woods at the point described previously, turn N just inside the E edge of the forest along a continuation of the bridleway. This will take you on a curving route through an area of forest known as Wytherston Wood, until eventually it brings you out at the NE corner of the forest alongside a disused railway track. Continue along the bridleway until it meets a tarred road. Turn right along this road for just under ½ mile; then turn right down a bridleway leading to Barrowland Farm. From this farm you return to the parked car by following the previous directions.

NOTE 2: Eggardon Hill, and most of the surrounding farmland, is used for sheep rearing, so on this part of the walk dogs MUST be kept on a lead.

Points of Interest
The "Fort". The low octagonal enclosure within the Eggardon ramparts, marked as a "Fort" on some Ordnance Survey maps, is in fact comparitively modern. It marks the site of a former coppice, planted as a seamark to assist mariners and fishermen — and also, so it is rumoured, smugglers!

Walk No. 18

The Lost Valley

Loscombe — Chandler's Coppice — North Poorton —
Hooke Park Forest — Coltleigh Farm — Loscombe
Distance: Approx. 9 miles.
O.S. Map: SY 49/59 (1:25000) or 194 (1:50000)

THE tiny hamlet of Loscombe lies hidden away
amongst high, turf-covered downlands, and some say its
name is an abbreviation of Lost Coombe — the Lost
Valley. Another theory is that it derives from a Saxon
word meaning "sheltered valley". Be that as it may, it is
so secluded that very few strangers ever find their way

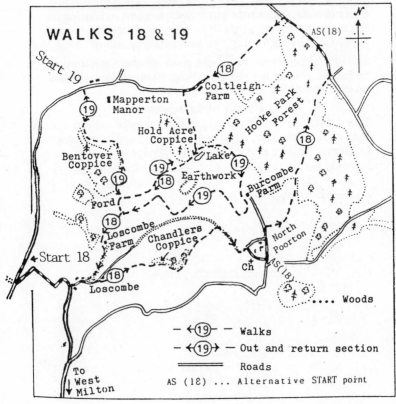

WALKS 18 & 19

Start 19

AS(18)

(18)

Coltleigh Farm

Mapperton Manor

Hold Acre Coppice

Hooke Park Forest

(19)

Bentover Coppice

(19)

(19)

(18)

Lake

(19)

Earthwork

(18)

Burcombe Farm

Ford

(19)

Start 18

Loscombe Farm

Chandlers Coppice

North Poorton

Ch

(18)

Loscombe

AS(18)

Woods

To West Milton

— ←(19)— — Walks
— ←(19)→ — Out and return section
═══ Roads
AS (18) ... Alternative START point

into this Dorset backwater — and even fewer discover the magic beauty of the wooded coombes which lie beyond.

To reach the starting point for this walk, make for Melplash on the A3066 Bridport — Beaminster road. Take the Mapperton turn-off opposite the Half Moon Inn. After ½ mile you will see a narrow lane on your right signposted "Loscombe". DO NOT drive down this lane as there are no parking spaces. Instead, head straight on a little further, where there are several convenient spots for grass verge parking.

From here it's a pleasant walk back down the lane into Loscombe. On reaching the stream at the bottom of the valley continue roughly E up a narrow lane marked with a blue and red "cul-de-sac" symbol.

Continue up this lane for about 400 yards, ignoring a turning off to the left. A little way beyond this left-hand turning you will see an opening on your right which gives access to a footpath. This leads you very pleasantly alongside a tiny stream into a grassy coombe.

After ½ mile you come to a waymark which indicates where the path crosses to the opposite bank of the "streamlet". From here you climb steadily upwards alongside a rather neglected strip of woodland called Chandler's Coppice, and eventually arrive at lonely Greenway Barn. Heading on NE, you soon come to an unsurfaced lane. Turn right along this towards the conspicuous spire of North Poorton church. Turn left just beyond the church along a tarred lane that runs due N for about ¼ mile. Where the lane eventually curves sharp left you should turn off to the right on to a small patch of wayside waste ground. A few yards distant, half-hidden by the undergrowth, you'll see a blue-arrowed waymark post and a gated bridleway which leads you up through a wooded, water-worn ravine.

At the top end of the ravine another gate leads out into a grassy field, beyond which rises the vast acreage of Hooke Park Forest. You must now bear away slightly to your left (direction NNE) towards a hedge. Follow this hedge until you come to a gate. Pass through this gate; then head on downhill along the *western* side of an out-jutting section of the forest. At the bottom of the slope (and well hidden among trees) there is a bridge across a small stream. This bridge carries the bridleway into the forest, and for the next 100 yards or so the hoof-churned path becomes rather muddy in wet weather. However, the ground is rising all the time, and soon the going becomes drier and a lot firmer.

From here the bridleway heads NNE through the forest, with plantations of beech and conifers predominating, and eventually it brings you out on to a tarred by-road.

Turn left along this road until you come to the NW corner of the forest. Just beyond this point you pass through a gate on your left which gives access into a grassy field. A bridleway heads W across the turf from this gate, and then curves SW to join up eventually with a farm track which heads on past Coltleigh Farm — a mellow old stone house with mullioned windows.

About 100 yards beyond the farmhouse you'll come to a pleasant green lane branching off downhill to your left. Your route lies down this lane, but before pressing on you should pause to admire the view. To the N an impressive belt of mature woodland clings to a steep hillside — a favourite hunting area for buzzards.

To the E you can look back upon the rolling green contours of Hooke Park Forest; whilst to the SE are the brooding heights of Eggardon. Almost due S is the distinctive outline of Shipton Hill.

The green lane heads steeply downhill into another deep, wooded coombe, and on arriving at the bottom you join up with a grassy bridleway that meanders away very seductively to your left and right. On this walk you turn right, but you can explore the left-hand route another day with Walk No. 19.

Down in the bottom of the coombe there flows a stream, and the chances are that your arrival in this lonely spot will disturb a heron fishing on its banks. Deer, too, are often to be seen along this path if you walk quietly.

Eventually you arrive at a spot where the wooded trail branches in several directions. You take the left-hand trail, passing close to a lonely ruined farmhouse; then, after crossing a ford, you head on down the valley to Loscombe Farm. The bridleway skirts the farm buildings, and soon brings you out into Loscombe hamlet. From here you retrace your steps to the parked car.

Walk No. 19
A Beautiful Backwoods Trail
Mapperton — Hooke Park — Burcombe — Burcombe
Wood — Mapperton
Distance: Approx. 5¾ miles.
O.S. Map: SY 49/59 (1:25000) or 194 (1:50000)

THIS lonely walk through a series of deep, wooded coombes is superb at any time of the year, but on a sunny day in spring it is sheer magic. It begins near the beautiful old manor house at Mapperton, and to reach this from Bridport you drive along the Beaminster road as far as Melplash, then turn right opposite the Half Moon Inn. Mapperton lies about 2 miles along this lane. For a modest fee (10p at the time of writing) you can use a parking space near Mapperton cottages. As a matter of courtesy, please do not park on the lawn-like verges in the hamlet itself.

Many Ordnance Survey maps corrected up to 1977 still show a bridleway passing in front of Mapperton Manor House, but this public right of way has now been diverted about 250 yards W, and its route through a gate and across a field is indicated by a laneside signpost.

After crossing this field you head towards a cottage on your right, and pass through another field gate bearing the notice: "Game Reserve — all dogs on lead, please". Your route now lies directly downhill, along the bottom of a grassy valley. Do NOT enter the private wood on your right.

Near the bottom end of this field the bridleway bears to the right, passing through an iron gate which has been badly bent by a falling tree. The track now runs along the bottom of the coombe, with the beautiful woods of Bentover Coppice rising steeply on your right. Deer are often to be seen hereabouts.

At the bottom end of this coombe you come to a sort of grassy glade, where several streams and trackways meet. Your route lies along a rising track which curves around to the left, and soon settles down in an ENE direction to lead you gently uphill into another wooded coombe. This is a very beautiful and solitary stretch of country where, in due season, a wide variety of wild life goes about its business of foraging, hunting, courting and breeding.

The track meanders steadily up the coombe into the lower SW corner of Hooke Park Forest; then turns abruptly S to emerge from the forest and head towards Burcombe. From here a footpath branches off from the bridleway and heads downhill into another wooded coombe which could be a twin of the one you have recently walked up. Indeed, the two valleys are only separated by a steep 413 ft hill that is crowned by a spectacular prehistoric earthwork.

Eventually the path emerges from the coombe and joins up with a bridleway. Turn right along this track, and soon you will come to a ford and the ruins of an abandoned farmhouse. You are now back in the glade you passed through on the opening stages of your walk, and from here you take the same route back to your parked car.

NOTE: It is also possible to begin and end this walk at Beaminster. A pleasant bridleway to Mapperton branches off to the E from the A3066 about ¼ mile S of Beaminster, crossing Coombe Down Hill, and passing beneath the Posy Tree. (See below). The return journey from Mapperton to Beaminster can be made along another bridleway which begins just W of the cottages in Mapperton, and joins up with the B3163 about ½ mile SE of Beaminster. Total extra distance: 3 miles.

Points of Interest
Mapperton Manor House. From the bridleway at Mapperton you obtain a good view of this mellow old stone manor house, which is generally considered to be one of the most charming and picturesque in Dorset. The terraced gardens are open to the public for a modest admission fee from 2 - 6 p.m. daily (March - October).

The Posy Tree stands beside the lane about ¼ miles W of Mapperton. In September 1666 the Great Plague reached its peak in Dorset, and beneath this tree the surviving villagers of Mapperton gathered with posies of herbs and flowers to ward off the plague while the bodies of the dead were taken up a side lane to a common grave on Warren Hill.

Walk No. 20

Lewesdon Hill

Distance: Approx. 4 miles
O.S. Map: Explorer sheet 116 or Pathfinder 1298 (1:25000);
193 (1:50000).

LEWESDON ("the Sheltered Hill") rises to a height of
892 feet, and from base to summit its steep slopes are clad
with beautiful woodlands of giant beech, ash, oak and pine,
with here and there a leavening of birch and rowan. There are
sunlit glades where, in due season, nature spreads a colourful
carpet of wild flowers; whilst on a sunny autumn day the hill
glows with the gold of falling beech leaves.

To reach Lewesdon, drive along the B3162 Bridport –
Broadwindsor road, and park on the wide grass verge just N
of Four Ashes cross-roads. The spot is marked on O.S. maps
as Buck's Head.

From here walk W along a concrete surfaced lane leading
to Brimley Coombe Farms, but after about 300 yards turn off
to the right through a waymarked gate on to a track that
climbs steeply up the wooded hillside. Before long, as you
gain height, the land drops away steeply on your right,
providing grand views through the beech trees of the Dorset
countryside spread out below.

On reaching a waymark post, ignore the indicated
bridleway leading off to your left, and instead continue
straight on and upwards along the footpath which soon brings
you to a National Trust sign. From here a little more climbing
brings you to the flattish summit, where the path forks to
follow the W and E edges of the small plateau.

Take the right-hand path along the E edge of the hill-top,
and continue to follow it when it broadens out into a track that
descends the N side of the hill. On nearing the bottom edge of
the tree-line it joins a bridleway, and here you turn left along
what was once an important route as far back as Roman times
and beyond, but which has now become sadly neglected.

Eventually this track leads out on to a farm access lane that is signposted: "Bridleway". Turn left along this lane for about 200 yards until it bends sharp right. Here you continue straight on through a gate into a pasture field. Follow a line of trees on your right, and then through a gate in the bottom corner. Beyond the gate turn left (SE) along a track that is trying hard to turn itself into a watercress bed!

Ignoring various farm tractor tracks which cross the bridleway, continue on roughly the same heading until the track makes a sharp left turn, and then another to the right. Immediately beyond the second bend you pass a small rushy pool on your left. From there on the lane becomes easy to follow, and after passing the Brimley Coombe farm buildings and cottages it brings you back to your parked car.

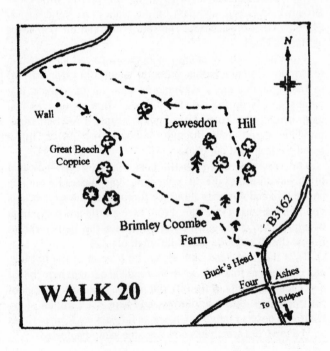